I0346946

This book belongs to

_____

* * ❋ * ❋ * * * * * ❋ *

Dear Amazing You,

Welcome to your spiritual journey of self-love!

As a teen girl, you're at a unique and exciting stage of life, full of possibilities and discoveries. But amidst all the changes and challenges, as you stand on the brink of so many possibilities, it's important to remember that the most significant journey you'll embark upon is the one within yourself.

Self-love isn't just a trendy phrase; it's an essential foundation for your happiness, confidence, and growth. It's about embracing who you are, not just on your best days, but every day. It's recognizing your worth, your strengths, and your unique beauty, both inside and out.

During your teenage years, you'll encounter many changes – physical, emotional, and mental. You'll face pressures from all corners: school, friends, family, and the ever-present social media. It's easy to get lost in the whirlwind of expectations and comparisons. But here's where self-love, through a deep connection with God, becomes your anchor.

Self-love is a powerful practice that will shape how you see yourself and how you interact with the world. It will allow you to see who you truly are, recognize your worth, and take care of your well-being.

© Copyright 2024 by Grace Walsh - All rights reserved.

The content contained within this book may not be reproduced, duplicated, or transmitted without direct written permission from the author or the publisher.

Under no circumstances will any blame or legal responsibility be held against the publisher or author for any damages, reparation, or monetary loss due to the information contained within this book, either directly or indirectly.

Legal Notice:

This book is copyright-protected. It is only for personal use. You cannot amend, distribute, sell, use, quote or paraphrase any part or the content within this book, without the consent of the author or publisher.

Disclaimer Notice:

Please note that the information contained within this document is for educational and entertainment purposes only. All effort has been executed to present accurate, up-to-date, and reliable, complete information. No warranties of any kind are declared or implied. Readers acknowledge that the author is not engaging in the rendering of legal, financial, medical, or professional advice. The content within this book has been derived from various sources. Please consult a licensed professional before attempting any techniques outlined in this book.

By reading this document, the reader agrees that under no circumstances is the author responsible for any losses, direct or indirect, which are incurred as a result of the use of the information contained within this document, including but not limited to errors, omissions, or inaccuracies.

Leave A Review!

Hey gorgeous!

Don't forget to share the love and leave your Amazon review for:

. . . .

Devotional Self-Love Journal for Teen Girls: A 21-Day Workbook to Foster Self-Esteem and Confidence through Scripture, Devotions & Prayer

You should know that life's challenges are more manageable
when you know how to be kind to yourself,
even when things don't go as planned.

Through this practice, you will learn to observe and understand
your emotions, as well as forgive yourself for
mistakes (after all, we all make them!), by reaching out to
God for inner strength, peace, and self-compassion.
You'll also learn how to set boundaries peacefully and
respect your needs. You will discover that you are not
defined by your achievements, your looks, or what others
think of you.
You are valuable just as you are – no matter what.

As you delve into this workbook, remember that self-love is
a journey, not a destination. Some days will be easier
than others. There will be moments of doubt and challenges
that test your resolve, but with faith as your greatest
ally, you will discover that God always has your back.

Every step you take on this path is a celebration of your
strengths, your dreams, your quirks, and even
your imperfections.

So, dear one, let's begin this adventure together.
Let's explore, learn, and grow in our love for God, and
love for Self.
Because you, exactly as you are, are worth loving.

Blessings,
Grace x

Through God, may you find peace.

May you give yourself the love you deserve.

—Y.D. Gardens

Week 1: Discovering Self-Love Through Faith

Day 1: What is Self-Love?

Self-love, especially for you as a teen girl, is like being your own best friend. It's about embracing who you are, with all your quirks, strengths, and even the things you might not be so fond of. It's like giving yourself a big, understanding hug, especially on days when things feel tough.

Imagine looking in the mirror and instead of focusing on what you wish were different, you smile and say, "Hey, I'm pretty awesome!" That's self-love. It's recognizing that you deserve kindness, respect, and happiness, just as much as anyone else, and then making sure you give those things to yourself.

Self-love is not about being narcissistic or thinking you're better than others. It's the opposite! It's about giving yourself the same compassion and care you'd give to a good friend. When you love yourself, you understand that making mistakes is part of growing up, and you learn to be gentle with yourself during those learning moments.

And the gentler you become with yourself, the more you will grow in kindness and compassion towards others.

In a world where social media and so many other influences can make you feel like you're not enough, self-love is your power, your shield. It helps you to stay true to yourself and not get swayed by unrealistic expectations or comparisons with others. It is the foundation that will allow you to grow into the best version of yourself.

Now, practising self-love encompasses many things. It includes taking care of your body, mind, and soul. It's about doing things that make you feel good, both short-term and long-term. These can include developing positive lifestyle habits like eating healthy, exercising, praying, pursuing hobbies, and spending time with people who make you feel happy and supported.

As you'll soon discover, self-love also involves learning say no when something doesn't feel right.
Finally, it is also about developing inner strength and extending that love, empathy and understanding towards others.

Cultivating self-love is a beautiful lifelong process. Some days will be easier than others, and that's okay. The important thing is that you keep moving forward, treating yourself with the love and respect you deserve. Your relationship with yourself sets the tone for every other relationship in your life, so make it a
loving and positive one!

How can my relationship with God help me learn to love myself, just as I am?

_____
_____
_____
_____
_____

Today, I am learning to love myself by...

_____
_____
_____
_____
_____
_____
_____

Day 2: Identifying Your Strengths

> A PRAYER FOR COMFORT AND GUIDANCE TO DISCOVER AND EMBRACE YOUR GOD-GIVEN, UNIQUE GIFTS.

Heavenly Father,

In the quiet of this moment, I come before You with an open heart. You, who have known me since before I was born, understand every part of my being. Today, I seek Your divine guidance to discover the strengths You have lovingly placed within me.

Lord, help me to see myself through Your eyes—beyond my doubts, fears, and the expectations of the world.

Illuminate the talents and abilities that You have uniquely bestowed upon me. Teach me to recognize the gifts that I may overlook, those hidden treasures that You have sown in the depths of my heart.

Grant me the wisdom to understand my strengths, and the courage to embrace them.

Let Your Holy Spirit lead me on this journey of self-discovery.

Help me to use these strengths not just for my own growth and fulfillment, but also to uplift others and to glorify Your name.

In moments of uncertainty or comparison, remind me of Your unconditional love and the special plan You have for my life.

May I always remember that my true worth and identity are found in You.

In the name of Jesus Christ, I pray,
Amen.

My Daily Intuitive Journaling

Chatting With God...

Remember, you are wonderfully made by God, reflecting His image and beauty.

"God created mankind in His own image."

Genesis 1:27

Day 3: Embracing Your Uniqueness

Embracing and celebrating your uniqueness is like nurturing a precious flower in a vast garden of diversity. Each one of us is wonderfully unique, with special talents, thoughts, and dreams that nobody else possesses.

It's important to remember that your individuality is not just what sets you apart, but it's also your strength. When you honor your unique qualities, you bring something different and valuable to the world.

In a society that often pressures you to fit in, daring to be yourself is an act of courage and self-love. Your unique perspective, your personal story, and your distinct talents are gifts to be cherished and shared.

So, celebrate who you are, for in your uniqueness lies your true beauty and power.

Remember, it's your differences that make you extraordinary, not just to fit into the world, but to help shape a better, more diverse, and inclusive future for us all.

Daily Thoughts: What makes me unique?

_____
_____
_____
_____
_____
_____

Dear God...

_____
_____
_____
_____
_____
_____
_____

Remember, you are wonderfully made by God, reflecting His image and beauty.

Day 4: Understanding Emotions

Understanding and managing your emotions is a vital part of your journey through adolescence - and life.

Emotions, like waves in the ocean, can sometimes feel overwhelming, swiftly changing from calm to turbulent. It's important to know that experiencing a wide range of emotions is completely normal and a sign of your growing awareness. Self-regulation is about recognizing these emotional tides and learning how to ride them gracefully.

This means taking a moment to pause, breathe, and reflect on what you're feeling before reacting. It's about finding healthy ways to express yourself, whether it's through talking to someone you trust, reaching out to God, writing in a journal, or engaging in a creative activity.

By understanding your emotions, you gain valuable insights into who you are and what matters to you.

Remember, your emotions are powerful tools for understanding your world and yourself. When listened to with care and respect, they can lead you to a deeper understanding of your incredible self.

Daily Thoughts:
What emotions did I feel today?

_____
_____
_____
_____
_____
_____

Dear God...

_____
_____
_____
_____
_____
_____
_____

Day 5: Setting Personal Boundaries

Boundaries are like invisible lines that define what is comfortable and acceptable for you, both emotionally and physically. They help you protect your sense of self and your well-being.

It's important to recognize that you have the right to set these boundaries and that doing so is a form of self-respect. Setting boundaries might involve saying 'no' to something you're not comfortable with, asking for personal space, or expressing how you wish to be treated by others.

It's okay to be clear and assertive about your limits, and it's equally important to respect the boundaries set by others. By understanding your own limits, you teach others how to treat you, and this leads to healthier and more respectful relationships.

As you grow and learn, your boundaries might shift and change, and that's perfectly normal. Just keep listening to yourself, and remember that your feelings and comfort are always valid.

These are things I choose to let into my life:

_____
_____
_____
_____
_____
_____
_____

These are things I do not want in my life because they don't make me feel happy and safe:

_____
_____
_____
_____
_____
_____
_____

"Be patient with yourself. Self-growth is tender; it's holy ground."

—Stephen Covey

Day 6: The Power of Positive Self-Talk

The power of positive thoughts and self-talk is truly transformative.

It's like nurturing a garden in your mind, where positive thoughts are the seeds that bloom into confidence, happiness, and resilience. Understand that the way you talk to yourself shapes your perception of the world and your place in it.

When you choose positive, encouraging words, you're not just being optimistic; you're building a foundation of strength and self-belief. This doesn't mean ignoring challenges or difficult emotions, but rather facing them with a mindset that says,
"I am capable, I am worthy, and I can grow from this."

Negative thoughts may visit like unwelcome guests, but remember, you have the power to escort them out and replace them with affirmations of your value and potential.

By practicing positive self-talk, you reinforce your abilities, celebrate your successes, and navigate your insecurities with compassion.

This habit not only uplifts you but also radiates outward, influencing your relationships and how you encounter life's journey.

Embrace the power of positivity within you, for it is a key to unlocking a world of self-empowerment and endless possibilities.

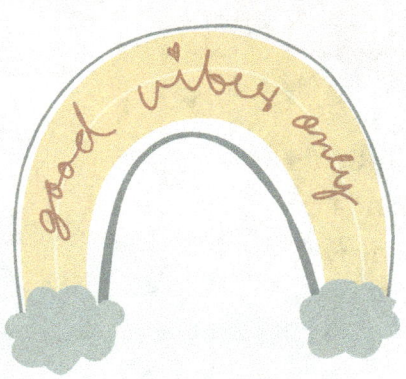

My positive self-talk sounds like...

Mistakes are stepping stones to success;
they teach me valuable lessons.

I am worthy of respect and love, and I treat myself with kindness and compassion.

Each day, I grow stronger and more confident in who I am and who I am becoming.

My voice matters, and I confidently express my thoughts and feelings.

I am surrounded by God's love and support, and I am empowered to reach my dreams.

My daily thoughts & feelings....

Dear God,

Day 7: Self-Love Rituals

Daily self-love rituals are like nurturing sunlight for your soul, vital for your growth and well-being.

These rituals are small acts of kindness you do for yourself, affirming that you are important and deserving of your own care and attention. Whether it's a few moments of prayer, journaling your thoughts, or simply enjoying a hobby that brings you joy, self-care habits are essential for building a loving and supportive relationship with yourself. They help you connect with your inner world, recognize your worth, and recharge your emotional batteries.

Remember, making time for self-care isn't selfish; it is the foundation upon which you build your strength and confidence.

By dedicating time each day to love and nurture yourself, you're not only enhancing your own life but also empowering yourself to bring your best to others.

So, cherish these moments of self-love; they are precious steps on the journey to discovering and honoring the wonderful person you are.

My favorite self-love rituals:

1. _____
   _____

2. _____
   _____

3. _____
   _____

4. _____
   _____

Dear God,

_____

_____

_____

_____

_____

_____

_____

You are God's masterpiece, created for a special purpose.

"For we are God's handiwork…"

Ephesians 2:10

Day 8: The Concept of Self-Esteem

Self-esteem is like a mirror reflecting how you view and value yourself. It's not just about feeling good; it's about acknowledging your inherent worth regardless of achievements or comparisons to others.

Healthy self-esteem means recognizing your strengths and accepting your weaknesses as natural parts of being human. It's understanding that your worth isn't measured by external factors like popularity, looks, or grades, but by the qualities that make you uniquely you - your kindness, resilience, creativity, and so much more.

To build self-esteem, you'll need to treat yourself with compassion, celebrating your successes, no matter how small, and learning from challenges without harsh judgment.

Remember, your self-esteem is a personal journey, one that flourishes when you treat yourself with the same love and respect you offer to others. Nurturing your self-esteem is one of the most important things you can do, as it sets the foundation for a confident, fulfilling life.

Self-Esteem Quiz

This quiz can help you reflect on how you feel about yourself and recognize areas where your self-esteem is strong and areas where you might need some extra support.

Remember, this is just for your own personal reflection and growth!

1. How often do you feel proud of your achievements, big or small?

A) Almost always   B) Sometimes   C) Rarely   D) Never

2. When you make a mistake, how do you usually react?

A) I learn from it and move on
B) I think about it for a while but eventually let go
C) I tend to beat myself up about it
D) I feel like a complete failure

3. How comfortable do you feel expressing your own opinions, even if they're different from those around you?

A) Very comfortable   B) Somewhat comfortable
C) A little uncomfortable   D) Not comfortable at all

4. Do you accept compliments easily?

A) Yes, I accept and believe them   B) Sometimes, but I feel awkward
C) Rarely, I usually doubt them   D) No, I don't believe them

5. How do you feel about your appearance?

A) I love the way I look   B) I'm generally okay with my appearance
C) I'm often critical of my looks   D) I really dislike the way I look

6. How often do you compare yourself to others?

A) Rarely or never   B) Occasionally   C) Quite often   D) All the time

7. Do you feel confident about your abilities and skills?

A) Yes, most of the time
B) Sometimes, depending on the situation
C) Not very often
D) Hardly ever

8. How do you handle criticism?

A) I take it constructively and learn from it
B) It depends on who's giving it and how it's delivered
C) It usually makes me feel bad about myself
D) It devastates me and ruins my mood

9. Do you feel worthy of love and respect?

A) Yes, always
B) In most cases, yes
C) Sometimes I doubt it
D) No, I often feel unworthy

10. How often do you engage in self-care activities (like hobbies, exercise, relaxation)?

A) Regularly
B) Sometimes
C) Rarely
D) Almost never

Your Score...

Mostly A's: High Self-Esteem
Mostly B's: Good Self-Esteem with Room for Growth
Mostly C's: Low Self-Esteem, Consider Working on Self-Love
Mostly D's: Very Low Self-Esteem, Seek Support to Build Confidence

Remember, this quiz is not a diagnostic tool. It's meant to help you reflect on your feelings and attitudes towards yourself.
If you find that you're struggling with self-esteem, consider talking to a trusted adult, counselor, or therapist.
They can provide support and guidance to help you feel more confident and self-assured. X

Stand firm in your values and beliefs. Integrity shapes your character.

Day 9: Overcoming Comparison

In a world often focused on comparison, embracing your uniqueness is a powerful act of self-love.

Remember, comparing yourself to others is like comparing apples to oranges – each of you is wonderfully unique, with your own strengths, challenges, and journeys.

It's important to acknowledge that everyone's path is different, and what you see on the surface often doesn't reflect the entire story.

Instead of comparing, focus on what makes you, you. Celebrate your individuality, the traits and talents that set you apart. Embrace the fact that there's nobody else quite like you, and that's something truly special.

The only person you should strive to be better than is the person you were yesterday.

God made you perfect, just as you are. In your uniqueness lies your strength and beauty.

Things that make me amazingly unique are:

1. _____

2. _____

3. _____

4. _____

Dear God,

_____
_____
_____
_____
_____
_____
_____

"Call to me and I will answer you and tell you great and unsearchable things you do not know."

Jeremiah 33:3

Day 10: Celebrating Small Wins

Recognizing and celebrating your achievements, no matter how small, is crucial because it builds your self-esteem and reminds you of your capabilities and strengths.

Each small win, whether it's acing a test, standing up for yourself, or simply getting through a tough day, is a step forward in your journey and deserves to be acknowledged and celebrated.

Gratitude journaling is powerful because it shifts your focus from what's lacking in your life to the abundance that's already present, fostering a mindset of positivity and contentment. This practice helps rewire the brain to recognize and appreciate the good things, big or small, leading to increased overall happiness and well-being.

Today, I am most grateful for:

1. _____
   _____

2. _____
   _____

3. _____
   _____

4. _____

Dear God,

_____
_____
_____
_____
_____
_____
_____

You are a marvelous creation of God. Celebrate your uniqueness.

"I praise you because I am fearfully and wonderfully made."

Psalm 139:14

Day 11: Developing Resilience

Developing resilience is key as it empowers you to bounce back from challenges and setbacks, turning them into opportunities for growth and learning.

This strength not only helps you navigate the ups and downs of life with more confidence, but also lays the foundation for a strong and adaptable mindset.

_____

_____

_____

_____

_____

I can build resilience by:

- **Embracing challenges as learning opportunities:** View difficult situations as chances to grow and learn, rather than insurmountable problems.

- **Cultivating a supportive network:** Find your tribe! Surround yourself with friends and family who offer encouragement and understanding, and don't be afraid to seek their help when needed.

- **Practising positive self-talk:** Replace negative thoughts with positive affirmations to boost your confidence and keep a hopeful perspective.

- Developing problem-solving skills: When faced with a challenge, break it down into manageable steps and seek creative solutions instead of feeling overwhelmed.

- Taking care of my physical and emotional health: Regular exercise, a healthy diet, adequate sleep, and mindfulness practices like meditation.

This week, I am learning to be more resilient by....

_____
_____
_____
_____
_____

Dear God,

_____
_____
_____
_____
_____
_____
_____

You are God's masterpiece, created for a special purpose.

"For we are God's handiwork..."

Ephesians 2:10

Day 12: Cultivating Self-Compassion

Self-compassion means treating yourself with the same kindness and understanding that you would offer a good friend, especially during times of struggle or failure.

It helps you navigate the challenges ahead with a gentle and forgiving mindset, reducing stress and increasing your overall emotional well-being.

_____

_____

_____

_____

_____

Today, I forgive myself for....

_____
_____
_____
_____
_____
_____

Dear God,

_____
_____
_____
_____
_____
_____

Day 13: Setting and Achieving Goals

Setting goals is essential as it provides a clear direction for your efforts and dreams, helping you focus on what truly matters to you. It will empower you to take control of your future, turning your aspirations into actionable steps while fostering a sense of accomplishment as you achieve each milestone.

8 steps to create your own fun & inspiring vision board!

Define Your Goals and Dreams: Take some time to think about what you want to achieve and how you want to feel in different areas of your life, such as school, hobbies, relationships, personal growth, and health.

Gather Your Supplies: You'll need a large poster board or corkboard, scissors, glue or pins, and magazines or printed images. Don't forget markers, stickers, or any other decorative items to personalize your board.

Collect Images and Words: Look through magazines or search online for pictures, quotes, and words that represent your goals and dreams. These can be images of places you want to visit, quotes that motivate you, or symbols of your aspirations.

Arrange Your Vision Board: Lay out your images and words on the board without gluing or pinning them down yet. Play with the layout until you feel it visually represents your dreams and goals.

Attach the Elements: Once you're happy with the arrangement, start gluing the pictures and words onto the board, or pin them if you're using a corkboard. This is where your vision starts coming to life!

Add Personal Touches: Use markers, stickers, or other decorative items to make your vision board uniquely yours. You can add your name, draw symbols, or decorate the edges of the board.

Place Your Vision Board Somewhere Visible: Hang your vision board in a place where you'll see it every day, like next to your mirror, above your desk, or near your bed. This visibility will keep your goals and dreams at the forefront of your mind.

Update Regularly: As your goals evolve and you achieve certain dreams, feel free to update your vision board. It's a living representation of your aspirations, so it should grow and change just like you do.

Ideas for my personal vision board:

_____

_____

_____

_____

_____

Dear God,

_____

_____

_____

_____

_____

_____

_____

You are chosen and precious in God's sight.

"You are a chosen people, a royal priesthood..."

1 Peter 2:9

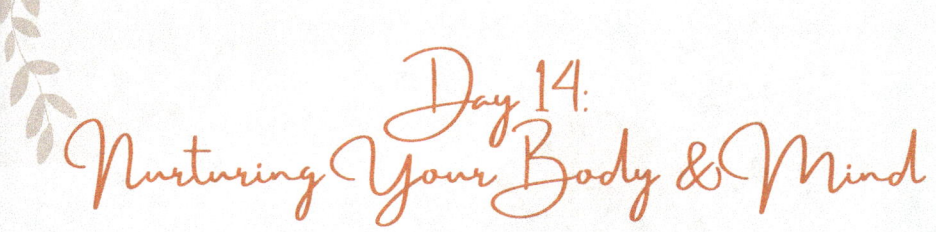

Day 14: Nurturing Your Body & Mind

Self-care is crucial because it's not just about taking care of your physical health; it's also about nurturing your mental and emotional well-being.

Regular self-care practices will help you manage stress, boost your self-esteem, and maintain a healthy balance in your life, ensuring you're at your best both for yourself and for others.

_____
_____
_____
_____
_____

My Self-Care Plan

♥ Physical Activity: Incorporate activities like yoga, dancing, sports, or simply going for a walk to keep your body active and energized.

♥ Healthy Eating Habits: Focus on a balanced diet rich in fruits, vegetables, and whole grains to nourish your body and mind.

♥ Mental Health Practices: Allocate time for activities that calm the mind, such as meditation, journaling, or reading a good book.

My Self-Care Plan

♥ Social Connections: Maintain healthy relationships with friends and family who support and uplift you, and don't shy away from seeking professional help if needed.

♥ Hobbies and Passions: Dedicate time to hobbies or interests that bring you joy and allow you to express yourself creatively, like painting, music, or crafting.

Embrace the strength and dignity with which God has gifted you.

"She is clothed with strength and dignity…"

Proverbs 31:25

Week 3:
Integrating & Applying Self-Love

Day 15: Connecting With Others

Building healthy relationships and connecting with others is vital as it provides a support system that can offer encouragement, understanding, and a sense of belonging.

These positive connections, whether with friends, family, or mentors, help in developing social skills, enhancing self-esteem, and navigating the complexities of life with more confidence and less stress.

_____

_____

_____

_____

8 Ways to Improve My Interpersonal Skills

<u>Active Listening</u>: Practice fully focusing on the speaker, showing interest, and not interrupting, to understand their perspective better.

<u>Body Language Awareness</u>: Be aware of your body language — maintain eye contact, use open gestures, and show that you're engaged in the conversation.

<u>Empathy Development</u>: Try to understand and relate to others' feelings and viewpoints, even if they differ from your own.

<u>Assertiveness Training</u>: Learn to voice your opinions and needs confidently and respectfully, without being aggressive or passive. Work on expressing your thoughts and feelings clearly and concisely, without mumbling or rushing your words.

<u>Conflict Resolution Skills</u>: Practice resolving disagreements calmly and constructively, focusing on finding solutions rather than assigning blame.

<u>Open-Mindedness</u>: Be open to new ideas and perspectives and willing to have your views challenged or changed.

<u>Feedback Reception</u>: Learn to accept and constructively use feedback, seeing it as an opportunity for personal growth.

<u>Patience and Tolerance</u>: Cultivate patience in conversations, especially when dealing with difficult or slow responses, and show tolerance for differing opinions and personalities.

This week, I will improve my interpersonal skills by....

_____
_____
_____
_____
_____
_____

Dear God,

_____
_____
_____
_____
_____
_____
_____

"You are braver than you believe, stronger than you seem, and smarter than you think."

A. A. Milne

Day 16: The Role of Social Media

The constant exposure to carefully curated and unrealistic images on social media can significantly impact your body image and self-esteem.

Remember that social media often showcases a filtered version of reality; focus on your own unique qualities and strengths, rather than comparing yourself to these idealized images.

_____

_____

_____

_____

My Social Media Detox Plan:

SET TIME LIMITS:
....
Allocate specific times for social media use to avoid excessive scrolling and ensure it doesn't interfere with important activities like studying, sleeping, or socializing in person.

FOLLOW POSITIVE ACCOUNTS:
....
Choose to follow accounts that inspire, educate, and uplift you, and unfollow or mute those that trigger negative feelings like inadequacy or jealousy.

ENGAGE ACTIVELY, NOT PASSIVELY
....
Rather than just scrolling, you can choose to actively engage by sharing content that reflects your faith, interests and values, and participating in meaningful discussions.

BE MINDFUL OF PRIVACY & SAFETY
....
Be aware of your privacy settings, think carefully about what personal information you share, and remember that online interactions should always be respectful and safe.

PRACTISE DIGITAL DETOXES:
....
Regularly take breaks from social media, whether it's for a few hours each day or a full day each week, to disconnect and focus on real-life experiences.

Release your worries to God, for He cares deeply for you.

"Cast all your anxiety on him because he cares for you."

1 Peter 5:7

Day 17: Exploring Creativity

Engaging in creative activities like drawing, writing, or playing music provides an outlet for self-expression and can be incredibly therapeutic. It can help process emotions and experiences in a healthy way, as well as foster a sense of accomplishment and joy.

Creative outlets will help you escape from the stresses of daily life and allow you to explore new worlds and possibilities within your own mind.

_____

_____

_____

_____

My Creative Outlets

- JOURNALING & CREATIVE WRITING
- SKETCHING & DRAWING
- PAINTING
- PHOTOGRAPHY
- CRAFTING
- DANCING
- MUSIC & SIGNING
- FASHION & DESIGN
- DIGITAL ART & DESIGN
- CERAMICS & POTTERY

My creative thoughts...

_____
_____
_____
_____
_____
_____

Dear God,

_____
_____
_____
_____
_____
_____
_____

God never forgets you; you are always in His thoughts.

"I will not forget you!"

Isaiah 49:15

Day 18: Mindfulness & Presence

Developing mindfulness helps to live in the moment. It also reduces stress and anxiety by focusing on the here and now, rather than worrying about the past or future.

Additionally, this practice enhances self-awareness and emotional regulation, leading to improved mental health, better concentration, and a deeper appreciation for the small joys of everyday life.

Sounds pretty perfect to me!

_____

_____

_____

_____

_____

5 Go-To Mindfulness Exercises

Deep Breathing: Spend a few minutes each day practicing deep breathing; inhale slowly through your nose, hold for a few seconds, and exhale slowly through your mouth. This helps calm your mind and focus your attention on the present moment.

Body Scan Meditation: Lie down in a comfortable position and slowly bring your attention to each part of your body, from your toes to your head, noticing any sensations or feelings without judgment.

Mindful Walking: Take a quiet walk, focusing on the sensation of your feet touching the ground, sounds around you, the air on your skin, and the sights you pass, fully immersing yourself in the experience.

Gratitude Reflection: Each day, take a moment to think of three things you're grateful for. This can shift your focus from negative thoughts to positive aspects of your life, fostering a sense of contentment.

Mindful Eating: During meals, focus on the taste, texture, and aroma of your food. Eat slowly and without distractions like TV or smartphones, to fully enjoy and appreciate your meal.

Your confidence comes from God's strength within you.

"I can do all this through him who gives me strength."

Philippians 4:13

Day 19: Future Self Visualization

Visualizing your future self is a powerful exercise that involves closing your eyes and imagining yourself in the future, picturing who you want to be, what you're doing, and how you're feeling in vivid detail.

This practice not only helps in setting goals and aspirations, but also boosts your motivation and confidence by creating a clear and inspiring vision of what you can achieve.

Letter to future self

Embrace the certainty of God's unfailing love.

"Nothing can separate us from the love of God."

Romans 8:38-39

Day 20: Community and Contribution

Community and family play a crucial role in our lives.

They offer a support system that provides love, guidance, and a sense of belonging, all of which are essential for healthy emotional and social development.

Being part of a community and having strong family ties can help you navigate the challenges, offering a safe space to learn, grow, and build lasting relationships.

Journaling about community....

How can I be more generous with others?

How can I support my family and friends?

"Those who are happiest are those who do the most for others."

Booker T. Washington

Day 21: Congratulations!

You've completed your 21-day journey of self-love!

So, what's next?

Well, as you now know, you are wonderfully unique and created in the eyes of God with special talents, thoughts, and dreams that nobody else possesses.

You must continue to embrace and celebrate your uniqueness, just as you would nurture a precious flower in a vast garden of diversity.

It's important to remember that your individuality is not just what sets you apart, but it's also your strength.

When you honor your unique qualities, you bring something different and valuable to the world.

In a society that often pressures us to fit in, daring to be ourselves is an act of courage and self-love.

On your journey, know that your unique perspective, your personal story, and your distinct talents are gifts to be cherished and shared.

So, celebrate who you are, for in your uniqueness lies your true beauty and power. Your differences make you extraordinary, not just to fit into the world, but to help shape a better, more diverse, and inclusive future for us all.

Thoughts & feelings....

_____
_____
_____
_____
_____
_____

Dear God,

_____
_____
_____
_____
_____
_____
_____
_____

Embrace the spirit of power and love given to you by God.

"For God has not given us a spirit of fear, but of power."

2 Timothy 1:7

My daily thoughts & feelings....

_____
_____
_____
_____
_____
_____
_____

Dear God,

_____
_____
_____
_____
_____
_____
_____
_____

My daily thoughts & feelings....

Dear God,

My daily thoughts & feelings....

Dear God,

"TO LOVE ONESELF IS THE BEGINNING OF A LIFELONG ROMANCE."

— Oscar Wilde

I'd love to hear your thoughts!

As an independent author with a small marketing budget, reviews are my livelihood on this platform.
If you enjoyed this book, I would truly appreciate it if you left your honest feedback.

You can do this by clicking the link to this Devotional Self-Love Journal for Teen Girls book on www.amazon.com.

www.ingramcontent.com/pod-product-compliance
Lightning Source LLC
Chambersburg PA
CBHW071219070526
44584CB00019B/3075